His Saving Grace:

A Reflection of Poems

By

Lenisha Tene White

White Boots 101 Writing Services LLC

Whiteboots101writingservicesllc.com

TABLE OF CONTENTS

3

Lenisha White is a believer, daughter, sister, educator and aesthete. Lenisha was born and raised in Mississippi and currently resides in Georgia. Before developing a passion for writing, Lenisha enjoyed singing. Like most, Lenisha grew up singing in the church then eventually started singing in talent shows, pageants, sporting events and weddings. From the beginning, writing was something Lenisha enjoyed. It became a coping mechanism when she would deal with difficult situations and challenging circumstances, but also became an outlet when things brought her joy. Everything that Lenisha writes about comes from a place of love. She is a product of grace and wants the world to know that we all are. Lenisha's goal is to connect with people through words because they carry so much power. Lenisha aspires to pour into souls. She wants people to know that they matter and that they're loved. Her prayer is for people to read her words, get a sense of who she is, what she's gone through, but mostly importantly see who **GOD** is and how great he is.

Gratitude to My Father

To my Heavenly Father from whom all blessings flow all glory, honor and praise belongs to You. I thank You for blessing me with this gift, You are such a kind and gracious God. As I sit and write this, I shake my head in laughter because I am quite sure You did the same thing. I can hear You saying, "This one right here, she doesn't get it now, but she will." I also sit here in amazement and awe of how I have been given such a gracious opportunity, You see something in me that I don't see in myself. However, You have taught me to believe in myself and to go after the great things that life has to offer. With You there is absolutely nothing that I cannot do. I have bumped my head so many times trying to figure things out on my own and trying to do things my way. You had to let me see YOUR power, You had to let me realize that no matter what You have me covered and you will remain the same. I ran from this for such a long time. I ran because of timing I felt like nothing was happening; that things weren't going in the direction that I thought they should be going in. I ran because I was scared and frustrated, I was intimidated by life and I compared myself to others. At times I was honestly being lazy putting it off to another day. I was incarcerated by fear and I also lacked confidence. There I was thinking to myself, "Who is actually going to read this?" I didn't believe that I had the connection so I was looking for the source in all the wrong places. You were the source all along, there were a million reasons as to why I didn't proceed with this. In reality I only needed one reason to actually do it. If I am an ambassador for you, if I am to be a vessel it requires obedience and sacrifice. The odds were definitely against me, I shed a lot of tears and wondered if you ever saw my pain and struggles. I became doubtful my faith waivered and that caused me to keep pushing this off, one minute I'm thinking, "Okay, I've got this. I can do this, I'm ready." I would be on a roll with trying to put everything together then, something would go wrong, or at least I felt like nothing was happening. Once again, my material would be sitting in the corner for days...months. I had no idea what was in my possession. I was constantly reminded to walk in dominion, to stand on your word and to trust and believe in your promises. This hasn't been the easiest journey, but I am so glad that You have been with me being my compass and my guide. It has been a journey, filled with many ups and downs, I am still learning to rely solely on You and not my own strength. I simply can't do this alone; I need You. Father, I thank You for choosing me. In the beginning, I didn't understand why of all people, You chose Lenisha Tene White. You knew the plans for my life before I even came into this world. There was a path set for me, without your guidance and direction- without your Grace and Mercy, I could not have done any of this. The path You set before me was preparation for what was to come. The obstacles of life, the hurdles and hardships were preparing me for this moment right now. You were lining me up for this position and it had a purpose, I have a purpose. I was built for this, because I am more than a conqueror. I am still in awe of You, God, You chose me and what a privilege, what an honor and I can never thank You enough. Looking over my life and seeing the ways You have made, the overcoming of trials and tribulations, moments of joy and sorrow, and even in the midst of despair, You were there all the time. You shielded me covered and protected me, You kept me when I couldn't even keep myself. It wasn't until now that I realized the calling You had on my life. Through my errors, bad judgment- my mistakes, You are still able to use me. I'm so unworthy, so unworthy, I am nothing but a filthy rag, chosen by the most-high God. Thank You for your forgiveness, thank You for another chance and allowing me to share my gifts and talents, I want to edify You, I want to glorify You. May your spirit continue to resonate in me, I am forever and eternally grateful to be a vessel, I desire to be an encourager and a witness of your glorious magnitude! I want to be used for your glory, thank You for the gift of life and your unconditional love. May everything that I do bring glory to your precious and holy name. Amen.

Your daughter, Lenisha

<u>Walking In Victory</u>

For years, living in silence

Afraid to face my fears

Many nights I sat alone

Shedding a fountain of tears

I couldn't see my way through

My life was torn into pieces

That is when my Savior stepped in

And gave me strength from within,

He picked me up wrapped me in His arms and said to me

Cry no more, I am here

What you have been longing for can only be found in me

This is your time

This is your moment

You are finally free

Go my child, Put your trust in me

This is your time

This is your moment to walk in Victory

You are not your past

I've captured You from your burdens

I am The One you call on when You are hurting

I am your Father, the keeper of your soul

I am that I am

Nothing can separate You from my love

I'm the greatest love story You have ever told

Remember, when I said that I will never leave You

Nor would I forsake You

I am a keeper of my Word

Take what I've shown You

And share it with those whose eyes have not seen

nor heard

Tell them of My goodness, tell them of My Grace

Tell them how You found joy in Me

by going into that secret place

That place of rest

That place of peace

That can only be given to You, from me

Tell them about your moment

That moment I set you free

How I saved You from yourself

All because You trusted in Me

You are now at a place of freedom

Gracefully walking in Victory

You went through the fire

You went through the storm and rain

It was my love- My grace and mercy

That kept you throughout the duration of your pain

Father, You freed me from my past

Looked beyond my faults

Still supplied my needs

That is what a loving Father does

He looks after His sheep

Lord, I heard Your voice time and time again

Saying, follow me, follow me

Let me

show You what life with me is about

You cast away all of my fears and doubts

The weight was finally lifted

I was finally set free

You picked me up,

changed my life and now I am walking in Victory

Never Alone

Who's going to love me with so many flaws?

Who's going to be there every time I call?

I call Him my Father, my Friend, my Savior

His name is Jesus

Never abandoned, never forsaken

I am anchored in His safety

His love for me can never be taken...away

Away from the noise and in tune with Him

He brings joy into my world when it seems so dim

Many nights I've laid awake

My mind wrestling

My heart hurting, heavy with ounces of pain

But Jesus came in

Gave me a sense of peace

When I felt that I could no longer sustain

The issues of life weighed heavily on my soul

I wanted to give up

I was becoming numb

Feeling nothing- becoming cold

But I felt His presence

I heard a still voice from Heaven

Saying, "My child, My child

Why are You worrying

You have Me, I am here

Your peace, your Comforter

The answer to your every concern

Take heart, I have overcome the world

I will lead you into a place where there is no harm

It is a resting place

A place where You will find peace-

A peace that surpasses all understanding Cast all of your cares upon me

His name is Jesus

The One who loves in spite of all of my flaws

The One Who is there every time I call

I have nothing to fret

I never have to worry

He's an on-time God

Who will come in a hurry

He never slumbers He never sleeps

He is my Protector

The one who keeps His loving arms around me

And keeps me in perfect peace

I am never alone

Angels

Never in my wildest dream

Did I ever think this would happen to me

On that day I took You away

Not knowing how it would affect me

Missing you, thinking of You

Wondering how your lives would be

I repented over and over again

Begging- crying out for forgiveness

Wishing I could undo what's been done

Life- what a precious and Beautiful gift from above

I look up to the sky

Envisioning your smiles

Bright and wide- quite similar to mine

And then You fade away

My mind goes back to the day that You went away

Oh, my sweet angels

My innocent, pure angels

I never wanted You to go away

We shall meet again someday

I love You

Oh, how I love You

I think of You each and every day

My angels, my loves

You were set free

Free to fly

Free to dance in Heaven

Forever in my heart You will be

I love You my sweet, beautiful angels.

In Due Season

God, where are You?

I've been calling your name

These tears I've cried

These prayers I've prayed

Still, nothing has changed

Everything is still the same

When is a change going to come?

I know there is a calm after the storm

But Father, I need You now

How much more of this do I have to endure?

I'm desperately waiting on You God, can you hear me?

My heart cries out for You

Lord, help me to see

There is better coming to me

It seems like my world is caving in

I've endured this race for so long

Tell me, when will I reach the end

I've stretched my hands to Thee

Crying out desperately for my breakthrough

People say You are only a prayer-call away

But it seems like I can't reach You God, don't

You see me? Have I not struggled enough?

I'm trying to keep the Faith

Trusting You at your Word

That You are always beside me when things get tough

How can I continue to go on

With my world shattering all around me?

I need that mustard-seed Faith

And remember that when I was lost

It was You who found me

In due season, I will reap my harvest

Right now, I am on Your time

You are a God who cannot lie

Whatever You have for me,

it will one day be mine

For now, I will rest in assurance

My current situation will enhance my endurance

To continue running this race

I simply have to rely on You

Doing it on my own strength is something

I cannot do

In due season, my Blessing will be waiting for me

I have no choice but to trust You

You are the Blesser who Blesses abundantly

If I ask, I will receive

If I seek, I will find

You are a God of perfection

You created time

An on-time God

That is who You are

In due season

my Blessing will be waiting for me

Lord, you will forever reign in Glory

Beyond what human eyes can see

You were there the entire time

You heard me, You saw me

I couldn't see it then, but I can see it now

It was all a part of your plan

For me to leave everything in the master's hand

So, your marvelous work could be revealed

I just had to hold on-- continue to be strong

For You are the Author and Finisher of my

Faith

Favor has been shown upon my life

You paid a price that I could never repay

This is it

My season is now

The journey has now begun

It wasn't until now that those three words

"in due season"

I fully understand I wasn't being patient with You

You were being patient with me

In due season you Blessed my soul

Once again, I can walk in Victory

Set Free

Fear, frustration, anger

This is what I am feeling

Lord, I need You now, more than ever

I'm in need of a healing

So many years of disappointment

And fleeing from your anointing

Not knowing the calling You had upon my life

selfishly

I wasn't willing to sacrifice

All along You had a plan and purpose for me

Things, people-- my judgment was clouded

And it didn't allow me to see

God, it was You who gave me the vision

All I needed to do was make the decision

My focus was on the negative

I couldn't see clearly of what was in front of me

Lord, it was You the entire time

You were there surrounding me

In all that was good, I could only see the bad But

You gave me hope and it surely made me glad

If it wasn't for your saving Grace, Where would I be?

Still fearful, frustrated and angry

And dying to be free

You placed something deep within my spirit

When I become full of doubt

I fall into prayer-- down on bended-knees

For I am one who the Son set free,

Therefore, I am free indeed

Battlefield

Abused, misused

Abandoned, confused

Betrayed blinded by love

Have I not suffered enough?

Fighting for my life,

Trying to sustain my sanity

Searching for what was never there, comfort, peace, civility

All while trying to maintain stability

A giver, never given too much

Hurt, deceit

Pain, defeat

Trying to find purpose in this pain

Down in the trenches

But my heart remained the same

The battlefield

Where so many wars take place In my mind,

my spirit, my soul

This is bound to happen to those with

"a heart of gold"

Broken promises

Less smiles, more tears

It has been a repeated cycle over the years

This battlefield –

images running through my mind

daydreaming of happiness Awaken by reality

Broken, battered

Accepting the past

Hoping for a promising future having "a heart of gold"

While living with a tired soul

Longing to be set free

I erase the pain from my memory

I can't let the enemy get the best of me

This battlefield-- danger, demons

One war after another

Trying to find a way to escape

How much more pain could "a heart of gold" take?

He came down and rescued me

This is the freedom that I desperately needed

Shelter and safety

The battle was finally over

I had been set free

Still a gentle soul with "a heart of gold"

No longer bound by attacks of the enemy

Power

Given away

Taken away

Either way, it was gone

My power, I felt, was out of my grasp

It was hidden deep within me like a treasure

Suddenly it was gone How could this be?

A special part of me

It resounds within parts of my soul

Blinded by my own desires Hypnotized by the charm

On that warm summer day

My power was taken away

Would I ever get it back?

Days, weeks, months, years—

I slowly began to fade

Losing myself to another human being

Entrapped, arrested by fear and emotions

Manipulation-- tricked into thinking it would get better

One day, I saw the light I had an epiphany

God began talking to me

We had a conversation

This was new to me

I became adjusted to conflict and confrontation

And not to my surprise,

God opened my eyes

He reminded me that I am fearfully and

wonderfully made

It wasn't about my physical attributes

It had nothing to do with my looks

I was created for a purpose

Handpicked-- chosen by The Most-High God

Not given a spirit of fear

My Heavenly Father is always near

He gave me a spirit of love, power and a sound mind

Now was the time—

the time to step out I am more than a conqueror

On that day, God placed His hands on me

He gave me the courage and strength

An overwhelming feeling came over me

I could not keep my composure

It was like a rebirth

This is where a new period of life began

My power was given back to me

No longer was I imprisoned

No more fear, no more insecurities,

spiritually and mentally

I was in a better place

Not done by my own strength

This was indeed a Blessing from God

My power was back in my possession

Transformed--pieces put back together differently

I am not the same

This is a different me

Words of Encouragement

People love to constantly remind us of who we *used* to be. For some,
it's hard to accept a drastic life change and not everyone will stay with
you on your journey. Everything has its season, so, surround yourself
with individuals who motivate and uplift you. You need individuals
who pray with you and for you. In doing so, speak over yourself, speak
over your life, proclaim your deliverance and proclaim your healing.
There is absolutely nothing wrong with asking others to pray for you
but remember that when you are having an open dialogue with God--
intimate conversations with Him is absolutely essential. For such a
long time I thought that praying big fancy words was the way for God
to hear me. I thought if I prayed this way and communicated that way,
He would understand what I was trying to convey in my prayers. God
isn't concerned about how well-spoken you are. He isn't looking for
eloquent words. He wants sincerity from your heart. If you don't know
the words to pray, ask Him and He will show
you.

*"And it came to pass, that, as he was praying in a certain place, when he ceased,
one of his disciples said unto him, Lord, teach us to pray, as John also taught his
disciples. And he said unto them, When ye pray, say, Our Father which art in
heaven, Hallowed be thy name. Thy kingdom come. Thy will be done, as in
heaven, so in earth. Give us day by day our daily bread. And forgive us our sins;
for we also forgive every one that is indebted to us. And lead us not into
temptation; but deliver us from evil."* **Luke 11:1-4**

We have all been judged, and honestly speaking, we have all judged one another. Upon coming into this new life, be ready, because the first thing that is going to be attacked, is your character.

You have to remember that you are no longer that person. You are not your past. You are not the mistakes you made. You are who *God* called you to be not what people CALLED YOU. We are His chosen people, those choices you have made in your past, have cultivated you into the person that you are now.

Look at how strong you are, you overcame it, you *are* more than a conqueror. Don't let the negative words of others dictate how you feel about yourself.

Most importantly, don't let them deter you from the path that God has set before you. He had a plan for you long ago. He knew the choices you were going to make (good and bad). But let me tell you about God's "Wonder Twins"-- **grace** and **mercy** I am so thankful for them. You don't have to walk with your head down. You don't have to continue carrying any guilt. He set you free, walk in liberty.

YOU ARE NOT YOUR PAST!

"This means that anyone who belongs to Christ has become a new person. The old life is gone; a new life has begun!" **2 Corinthians 5:17**

Win

The odds stacked totally against me

But I must stand strong

My Faith tested

Giving up is not an option

I have to remember that I will not lose

My Heavenly Father is always near

He forever stands by my side

The enemy wants to see me lose

He is always attempting to steal, kill and destroy

I find perfect peace in Christ Jesus

It is Him who bring me great joy

Continuously, I will stand tall, courageous and strong

I was born to win

Christ defeated death

He took up that Cross for me

I am the Daughter of The Almighty King

He placed something special within me

What I possess, can only be given to me by

the Most- High God

Faced with adversity-- challenges

I've seen so many walks of life

I will never give up

I will never give in

Placed here for a reason I am here to win

The word "can't" is no longer in my vocabulary

No longer will I say what I "can't" do

Difficulties, obstacles, challenges—

I trust God for my breakthrough

Sometimes it takes us falling into despair.

Experiencing some dark places

God is always showing His healing power

He sets free with His saving Grace

Never give up, Never give in

Tears may fall

But do not doubt what God can do

He performs miracles

There is nobody greater

Continue to look to the hills

Pray like you've never prayed before

God can open those closed doors

Trust in Him with all of your might

Remember, we walk by Faith--not by sight

It is only a test

This is not the end

Stay the course and persevere you were born to win

His Saving Grace

A life filled with so many different experiences

Searching, wishing, hoping--praying

My world turned completely upside-down at times

Storms, rain

The anticipation of wanting to be saved

Wanting to reach that point of redemption

My experiences positioned me

Who I am now is totally different from who I was

before

It took me hitting rock bottom

And accepting God's full control

I'm not in charge of my life

That is the role of my Heavenly Father

He did give me free will

Therefore, I have a choice

I've grown in my walk

When He speaks, I listen to Him

I am the sheep who knows His voice

Earlier in my life, my disobedience caused me to turn away

Going in the wrong direction

But He showered me with His love and saving Grace

Lost, living a life full of sin

How did I allow it to get that far

I used and abused my free will

Every excuse was made

Carelessly going about life

The seeds I had planted

Would one day be sown

I remember a quote that says'

"Grace is not a license to sin."

That is exactly what I did

I took God's Grace for granted

So many choices, selfishly made

Still, He looked beyond my faults

I am undeserving of His goodness

But again, I am covered by His blood and His saving grace

Blessings bestowed upon me daily

While I constantly fall short of His Glory

My thoughts and actions unpleasing in His sight

Fighting temptations day and night

Giving in to the pressure

I could've been left where I was

But my Father did not let me stay there

His love for me allowed me to receive another chance

Guilty of my actions

He corrected me of my wrongs

It was His saving Grace

That has kept me all along

His Grace-- that unmerited favor

It's not what I deserved

I haven't earned it

I can't earn it

Bearing that old-rugged Cross

Confessing Him as my Savior is what set me free

In more ways than one

I have been redeemed

There has been much deliverance

I have experienced freedom

No longer bound-- chains broken

Accepting His plans for my life

Spiritually and mentally, I am in a better place

It is He who has kept me

I am eternally Grateful for His saving Grace

Waiting

Anticipation, Eagerness, Excitement

This is what I'm feeling

My stomach churning

It's such a funny feeling

I know that God is up to something

But I have no idea what it is

I'm praying that it will soon be revealed

Seeking, searching

Trying my best to hold on

Everything that should be going right

Always ends up going wrong

Father, I'm waiting

I don't know how much more I can take   I'm in need of a miracle

Please make a way for me

Every direction I go in

The enemy is there, ready to attack

Here I am Father

Waiting-- waiting to hear a "yes" from You

Trying my best to walk in obedience

Although I am tired,

I've come too far to quit

I'm reminded of your Holy Word,

You will never abandon me

I will not be forsaken

Father, I'm waiting

I will work diligently and eagerly

While staying in Your will

Your will, let it be done

Let Your power fall

Perform a miracle in my life

Forever I will praise Your Holy name

You are the most-high God

The One who never changes

When I am weak, distressed--wanting to give you

You still remain the same

We have not because we ask not

Father, I'm asking-- praying-- pleading for

Your help

I know that my waiting is not in vain

You are about to do something so grand in my life

I will stand tall in Your Glory

I am doing it all for Your Glory

Father, if at any point during the test

You see me fading

Please reach down and touch me

Give me the strength to carry on

I know that it won't be very long

Before You give me the desires of my heart

Father, I am waiting

There is favor upon me

I shall be restored from the broken and shattered

pieces of my life

You are going to put me back together

I will be made whole again

Thank You for this season of waiting

It wasn't always easy

But I can do all things through

Christ Jesus who gives me strength

Smile

The world is watching- smile

Put on your big, bright smile

You're crumbling-- smile

Put on your big, bright smile

You're tired-- smile

Put on your big, bright smile

You're so angry-- smile

Put on your big, bright smile

You're in so much pain-- smile

Put on your big, bright smile

You're struggling-- smile

Put on your big, bright smile

The guilt-- keep smiling

Keep showing your big, bright smile   The

shame-- keep smiling

Keep showing your big, bright smile

*The embarrassment-- keep smiling   Keep showing your
big, bright smile*

The suffering-- keep smiling

Keep showing your big, bright smile

Smile-- that is what I taught myself

From the outside, looking in

No one could tell what was going on within

I used my smile as a cover-up

It was my shield-- the protector I needed

But my heart was bleeding

Trying to mask the pain and emptiness was not an easy task

I had to put on a brave face

Show the world that I have what it takes   There was

nothing to prove to the world

What I needed to do was live in my truth

Be honest about my reality

Because in all actuality

I was a broken soul

So instead of forcing the smile

I lifted my hands

Held my head up high

And gave God my deepest cry

My crying turned to Praise

My Praise turned to Worship

Then there was a shift in my spirit

It wasn't just something that I could feel

I could hear it

At that moment, I began to smile

It was bigger and brighter than ever before

This smile was different

It was genuine

Any inkling of doubt had dissipated

My Faith had been restored

Now when I am going through a tribulation—

When I'm in my valley

I remember The One who set me free

And lift up Holy hands and smile

Because I have the victory

<u>Nobody Knows</u>

Nobody knows my pain

Nobody knows my struggles

The pain I endure is something your eyes cannot see I

often ask myself

"Why do I feel all of this hurt"

"Why does this keep happening to me"

I know that I haven't lived the most perfect life

I've done many things that I'm not proud of

All I know is that I have to keep my head up

And continue sending my prayers up to

The One above

He is the only one who knows my struggles

He is the only one who can heal my pain

When the world has its back turned on me

I continue to give Him the highest praise

And forever call His precious name

I'm going through so much

I don't want the world to know it

I put on my big, bright smile

That way I don't have to show it

Throughout this life of mine

I've experienced many things

Did things I shouldn't have done

Said things I shouldn't have said

Saw things I wish I'd never seen

It hasn't always been easy

And it hasn't always been tough

Sometimes I just want to break down

Because I felt I'd had enough

But I cast my cares on someone who

I knew wouldn't fail me

He is the strength of my heart

He is the strength of my life

And I know He will always take care of me

Nobody knows my trials and tribulations

Hopefully there will come a time when I can tell my revelations

Sometimes I just want to run away

Run away to a land that's far, far away

I want to be free from my troubles

I want to live my life the right way

I'm not getting any younger

I'm only getting older

I want to release all of my burdens

I want to take this weight off my shoulders

The only way for me to truly be free is

to get my life in order

My days on earth aren't getting longer

They're only getting shorter

Sometimes I don't feel my best

But I'm going to continue to hold on and be strong

Because I know something great is in store for me

There are moments when I feel sad and blue

Because of broken promises that were made to me

I've been lied on, lied to—

mistreated, misused and I've been abused

I was left out in the cold for such a long time

So, lost-- so confused

I know there's going to be a brighter day

I will finally have things going in God's intended way

Until that time comes,

I will continue to hold on to my Faith

And I will continue to be strong

I will aim to please The Highest

And hear the words "Well done"

Nobody knows my struggles

Nobody knows my pain

But I know that as long as I continue to call His name

Receiving all of His Blessings will be my greatest reward to gain

Compass

Here she is,

I am here

Here I am

Who am I?

Where have I been?

What was I doing?

What made me

leave and just disappear?

Isolation-- the resolution to all of her problems

Needing time to think-- time to escape

The bad thing about it is that she spent more time on

self-hate

She didn't love herself

Focusing on everything that was wrong with her

Shattering what little confidence she did have within herself

Trying to find balance in her life

Everything was taking its toll on her

She wanted to feel some aspect of freedom

She wanted to find solace and peace

But all she focused on were the parts of herself that she

didn't like

Even though she's not superficial

She would always revert back to the physical

How could someone with a such a loving and giving heart

Not love herself and give into what society calls "beauty"

On the outside looking in

You would think there's so much confidence-- so much strength

But inside, she was falling apart

Trying to put these pieces of her life back together

Wanting to get back to that happy place

Not hiding behind smiles and laughter

None of it was real

A facade is all it was

Who was she before all the self-torment began?

She was vibrant, full of life

Strong-- a conqueror-- a warrior

Ambitious-- believing and aspiring to be someone great

Until one day, life knocked her down

Trying to fight her way back was one of the hardest struggles of her life

She tried and she tried with all of her might

Constantly trying to reach that point of victory

Distractions and delays

Partaking in things that ultimately shifted her way of thinking

Going left, when she should've gone right

Her sense of direction was gone

She lost sight of her guiding light

All it took was one touch of her Father's hand

What she needed was right in front of her

It gets difficult to see clearly when your judgement is cloudy

She knew she needed a way out

And the only way was through Jesus--her compass--her guiding light

She made peace within herself

He transformed her and changed her life

So now when things become too much to bear

And she can't see her way out She calls on The One--her compass-- her guiding light

Suicide

Just disappear she thought

It's much easier to be free from the pain Desperately

wanting to be immune from the circumstances at hand

Sleepless nights, restless nights

Tossing, turning

Agitated, frustrated

Crying out-- begging and pleading

But no one was coming to her rescue

She looked to her right, and saw something

It looked like the final solution

This would erase the bad memories

It would numb her

No more would she have to deal with everything stacked against her

She reached for what she thought was the final solution

Ironically, both were pain relief

Thinking back to the very beginning when it all started

And how life had taken its toll on her mentality,

spirituality and physicality

Every thought in her mind came from a very deep and dark place

She felt she couldn't even pray her way through this horrific storm

Her body weak and fragile

She felt lifeless and wanted to peacefully sleep away

Years and years of silence

Painting a false portrait

No one could see the depth of her suffering

One container in her left hand

In her right hand, there was the other

The only thing left to do was follow the instructions

Not the instructions on the label

But the ones she'd made for herself

Before she could proceed to take action

There was a still, quiet voice

It whispered to her, "This is not where your life ends.

This is where it begins."

Better

Alone, distraught, disheartened

Wondering, when will things get better

Faithless, furious filled with anger

Contemplating if it's worth it

To undergo such great ordeals of pain

The suffering—how much more can I bear?

I just want things to get better

I've hid behind my smile for so long

But I am at the point of breaking

Trying to gather up the strength to fight

I want to be like David—conquer these giants

And make them fall

These giants come in more ways than one

I can't do this alone

I need the help of The Holy One

He knows how to make things all better

A life filled with darkness and despair— torment, torture

Wondering how I would make it through

How much more can I bear

Countless times engaging in thoughts of ending it all

Life didn't seem worth living

Issues back-to-back

Life was becoming too chaotic

Filled with much distress

Would things ever get better?

It just seemed impossible

Deeper into depression, I fell

But His hands were still upon me

Crying out but no one could hear the sounds

Silent tears-- outside, they were not visible

But inside, flowing like rivers and oceans

I could have drowned in them

My Savior stepped in

With one finger, He gently wiped the tears from my eyes

His touch was so powerful

Who could do such an incredible thing?

At that moment, I felt His spirit

It was a sense of peace

Better is how I begin to feel

A weight was lifted

My train of thought shifted

Things got better once I fixed my thoughts on Him

A clear mentality

Satan thought he had me

Spiritually on a new level

I'm reminded when things get tough

They also get better

Troubles don't last always

There will be better days

For every mountain

For every hill and valley

There is a breakthrough

An abundant Blessing awaits you

Once I was Faithless, doubtful, disheartened

I was angry and confused

Now the anger has turned to delight

Out of darkness, came beautiful light

No more distress

No more silent tears

God has calmed my doubts and fears

I no longer worry about my stormy weathers

For He is The One who makes all things better

Redemption

Turmoil, distress, strife

Knocked down by life

Trying to figure out why I keep falling

One moment of triumph   The

next, a loss

Freedom is what I desire

The freedom to live without fear and regret

The freedom to live for Christ

Live the life that was meant for me

I was lost in the wilderness

Trapped-- captured by worry, guilt and embarrassment

I was chained to a life where I couldn't be who I wanted to be—
Who God called me to be

Thinking that my life wasn't worth living

I wanted to spread my wings and fly

Disappear from all of the madness that was going on in my mind

I needed an escape

I turn left, faced with life's adversities

67

I turn right, challenged with life's demands

Desperately wanting to grasp freedom

I lifted my hands

Choosing to let go of what was out of my control

I chose life

I chose freedom

The shackles that tried to restrict me from a life of abundance were

released-- they were no longer holding me

I chose to take charge of my destiny

I knew that I couldn't do it alone

I needed the help and guidance of my Savior

It was He who gave me unmerited favor

Life can easily knock you down

And you began to question every waking moment

There were no guarantees of this life without misfortune- tragedies

These are the things that make us strong

I had to endure the race

Fight the good fight

All while trying to maintain my Faith

Nothing was going to keep me at a place of defeat

I serve The Almighty King

It is He whom dwells in me

I was determined to rise above

I was built for this

And He reminded me that I never had to walk alone

In my times of weakness

It was my Father that I called

And that is when the giants began to fall

I went in, not knowing what the end would be

But I came out a winner-- a champion

Everything that I lost, was given back to me

I had been redeemed

Fighter

I've had to fight

Fight back tears

Fight for my life

Fight for my freedom

Fight for my peace, joy and strength

Frail, afraid-- almost destroyed

But I am a fighter

Everything that was meant to break me, and tear me apart

Only made me stronger and gave me much more heart

I've had to fight

Fight for positions

Fight depression

Fight suicidal thoughts

Fight to keep my sanity

I am a fighter

Almost defeated, almost destroyed

It was His saving Grace that kept me

Because of Him I was restored

I've had to fight

Fight against my enemies

Fight against my abuser Fight the anxiety

Fight all of the confusion

I've had to fight

Fight with my voice

Fight with my words

Fight with my Prayers

Fight with my sword-- God's Holy Word

When I thought I could not win It was His voice that I heard

I am a fighter

I've had to fight-- fight through this spiritual warfare

Fight my flesh

Fight to stay walking in the Spirit

Fight to follow His commands

I am a fighter

I've had to fight

Fight demons

Fight jealousy, envy and anger

Fight making hasty decisions

Fight putting my life in danger

I am a fighter

I've had to fight

Fight feeling worthless

Fight not feeling good enough

Fight my insecurities

Fight not giving in when things got tough

I am a fighter

I've had to fight

Fight abandonment

Fight being used

Fight being unappreciated

Fight being taken for granted

Fight being betrayed

With so much fighting, came so much strength

The strength to endure and persevere

*I am not **just** a fighter*

*I am not **just** a conqueror*

I am an overcomer

I am an achiever

No matter how many more fights come,

I know I will win Because I am a Believer

Words of Encouragement -Forgiveness

This is undoubtedly one of the hardest things to do. Whether it is forgiving others or forgiving yourself. When it comes to forgiving others, it isn't just for them. It is also for you. Carrying a grudge and harboring hatred will not get you anywhere. It robs you of your peace. You will be in a place of anger and misery. We love to say "Well, I can forgive, but I will never forget". Nobody is asking us to forget. There are a lot of things that I wish I could forget-- block and erase from my memory, and never think about again. I know that it takes a lot to forgive after being hurt, betrayed and humiliated. God instructs us to forgive *"If you forgive those who sin against you, your heavenly Father will forgive you. But if you refuse to forgive others, your Father will not forgive your sins."* Matthew 6:14-15 (NLT)

When we confess and ask God to forgive us for doing and saying things that aren't pleasing in
His sight, we're forgiven. He doesn't hold it over our head. It's not thrown in our face.

Then he says, "I will never again remember their sins and lawless deeds." **Hebrews 10:17 (NLT)**

I'm not asking you to be God when it comes to forgiving others. However, we are to be Christ-like. It's imperative to do things in a Godly manner. I know that when you're hurt, you don't think about anything else. We are imperfect people, we're human, what they did to you is not okay but we are to act in love. Remember that love is patient and kind and God has been patient with all of us, myself included.

"But when you are praying, first forgive anyone you are holding a grudge against, so that your Father in heaven will forgive your sins too." **Mark 11:25 (NLT)** Forgiveness can free us of so many things, forgiveness brings restoration and healing, and it can allow you to move forward peacefully. Not only did I have to forgive others, but I had to ask others for forgiveness. It doesn't just work one way because you can easily find yourself on the receiving end. I also found myself having to forgive Lenisha, I had to forgive myself for a lot of things that I didn't even recognize were having such a huge impact on my life. There was so much weight that I was carrying around. I carried it for so long, unaware that it could possibly destroy me spiritually, mentally, physically and

emotionally. Not forgiving others robs you of your freedom, peace and happiness. Take time to reflect and ask yourself is it worth it. Is it worth risking losing the people you care about? Is it worth putting your relationship with God in jeopardy? You have nothing to lose and everything to gain. Forgiveness allows us to move forward in peace and harmony.

"So, watch yourselves! If another believer sins, rebuke that person; then if there is repentance, forgive. Even if that person wrongs you seven times a day and each time turns again and asks forgiveness, you must forgive." **Luke 17:3-4 (NLT)**

"Get rid of all bitterness, rage, anger, harsh words, and slander, as well as all types of evil behavior. Instead, be kind to each other tenderhearted, forgiving one another, just as God through Christ has forgiven you." **Ephesians 4:31-32 (NLT)**

"Make allowance for each other's faults and forgive anyone who offends you. Remember, the Lord forgave you, so you must forgive others."

Colossians 3:13(NLT)

Freedom

When you can look back over your life

Thinking about all of your experiences

Reflect on the choices you've made

Look at where you started and where you are now

What you didn't have then

You have it now

The experiences brought about a change

Good and bad experiences taught you valuable lessons

Giving you a totally different perspective on life

Allowing you to appreciate your life and the people in it

Granted, there were some that had to go

Some by choice, others by force

The experiences, the choices-- there was hurt, happiness

Moments of joy and peace involved

Some anger, frustration and stubbornness

It's difficult letting go of who and what we think we need

It's really just a want-- most of the time, it's our flesh

Only Christ knows our needs

Even when He convicts us and corrects us

We try to find ways to justify and validate things

But our God is Gracious and kind

Remember when you first started your journey?

Remember when you rededicated your life to Christ?

You began your new walk

There was a time when you wouldn't dare be caught praying

Or reading your Bible and quoting scriptures

You had a reputation to maintain look at You now!

You're praying, praising, singing and shouting

Crying out His Holy name Your life has changed

You are no longer the same

The things that used to upset you,

Don't upset you anymore

You're no longer bound

No more resentment

No more hatred and unforgiveness

You have a new attitude

Full of boldness-- you're fearless

The Holy Spirit leads you

In your decisions, you consult with Him

It is the Father who leads and guides you

It is His direction that gets you to

where you're supposed to be

You're no longer second-guessing

He gives you that perfect peace

This is what freedom feels like

Your past no longer bounds you

You have been set free

All these years of sinful living

Chained, shackled--arrested in worldly living

It came to an end

Now you appreciate life

Wisdom and knowledge, you have gained

Instead of engaging in impure thoughts—

lustful desires, sexual immorality

You desire the Word of God

Your soul desires to be fed

You don't follow your heart

For it can be deceptive

It is the Holy Spirit in which you want to be led

By His stripes, you are healed

Through Him, you are saved

With repentance comes forgiveness

Then comes deliverance-- healing

Being able to move forward

This is what freedom feels like

Thank God for His saving Grace

<u>Love</u>

A sacrifice made

A high price paid

Pain and suffering endured

Nails placed in His hands and feet

He laid down His life for a sinner like me

His head bloody from a crown of thorns

He endured this pain while thinking of me

I am not worthy

But he thought I was worth saving

Who else would lay down their life for me

Nobody but You-- my Father, my King

That's love

The betrayal, the deceit

You already knew

Yet and still, you chose to forgive

My shortcomings, my disobedience

I've intentionally done wrong

Yet You still look past my faults I look at all the ways

You have made for me

Still, deliberate disobedience,

Yet and still, You continuously Bless me

Your grace and mercy have kept me

You love me because that's who you are

The cross you carried

On it, you were hung

You bled and you died

You rose again

So that I could have the right to the tree of life

I was born into sin but because of You, I can live again

In You, I do live, move and have my being

That's love I don't deserve it

Salvation-- Given from You to me

I've been set free

Changed, delivered

Shackles are no longer holding me

Your love is the greatest love of all

Thank You for accepting me

The ultimate sacrifice

The agony endured along the way

Silence-- no words spoken

Your love allowed You to bear the pain

Who can love me the way that You do

Selfless, unconditional

Great is Your love

Your love brings joy and peace Lord, thank You for receiving me
Thank You for Your undying love for me

Missing You *Dedicated to my Grandmother in Heaven*

The day you left was unexpected I couldn't believe it

I was hysterical

I didn't know what to do

How could this happen

And how could this happen to someone like you

For a moment, my world went blank

It's like I drifted into another land

My mind was bewildered and I couldn't understand

I was confused

I was lost

I didn't want to believe what was going on around me

I thought I would never have joy again

because of what was surrounding me

The sorrow, the hurt, the tears

The echoes of another one's cry

With the life you lived

I never expected you to die

At least not so soon-- not so suddenly

It seems like yesterday that you were just hugging me

Just hearing you call me "Sweet Thang" was enough

to make my face light up

All throughout life, you told me always be encouraged and never give up

Those words continue to remain instilled in me,

Even though you're not here anymore

Oh, how I wish you would just walk through that door

If it's just to say

"Hi, I'm still here and I'm always watching over you"

I know if you were still here there's nothing you wouldn't do

There were many nights when

I would cry myself to sleep

Asking myself over and over again

Why did He take you away from me

Couldn't He have let you stay here

just a little longer

Maybe I'm being selfish

I wanted you to stay forever

But I know that death is a part of life

And some things just don't last forever

I know time is something I will never get back

All I have are pictures and memories

And remembering how good you were to me

You were more than just my Grandmother

You were a sacred friend to me

If I could relive this moment all over again

I wouldn't change a thing

You're my precious Grandmother

And even though you're not here anymore

You still mean the world to me

I don't want you to be here—

just to suffer all over again

I can't help but to remember the day that you left

But I know you're in a better place smiling down on me

And in God's arms, you are safely kept

Grandmother, you will never be forgotten. I love you.

Your Granddaughter, Lenisha (NeNe)

<u>Mother</u>

Your love

Your sweet, gentle spirit

Your kind, caring soul

The sacrifices you continuously make

The road hasn't been easy

But with the help of the good Lord

You were able to provide us with a decent life

We may not have had a lot

But God brought us from such a long way

You worked hard day and night

Doing your very best, not getting enough rest

I don't tell you enough how much I appreciate you

I love you dearly

You are my greatest Blessing

Every day I thank God for you

I can't describe how much I love you

and all that you mean to me

I've watched you go through so much hurt and pain

I've watched you struggle

I've witnessed your smiles

I've also witnessed your tears

Seeing God work in your life gave me hope

Although I'm the child

It made me proud

It takes a lot of strength and courage

To get through your experiences

With God, all things are possible

You are evidence and living proof

My entire life, you have not only been a Mother

You played a two-parent role by yourself

I know it was a difficult task

You are woman of many hats

I'm Blessed to be your Daughter

Blessed to be your child

Thank you for your support and guidance

You are the epitome of a sacrificial Mother

You give your last

Selflessly putting our needs before yours

God could not have given me a better Mother

You are my Blessing

You are my champion

The one who withstands every obstacle

You are clothed in so much strength

Sometimes I think to myself

"How in the world does she do it?"

It's nobody but God

He has definitely smiled on you and your life, Mother

I thank you; I've learned so many valuable lessons

The most important one is to rely on God for everything

Mother, I love you

You are my greatest gift from above

You've shown me what it means to love

Mother, I appreciate you

And everything you've done for me

I adore you

Your meek and gentle soul

As a young child, I secretly never wanted you to get old

I'm cherishing our moments here on Earth

I never want to go a day without telling you that

I love you

My greatest joy is seeing you happy—

watching you smile

One of my main missions in life, has been to make you proud

Mother, I love you.

You are everything to me.

Your Baby Girl, Lenisha

Dear Mom,

I write this with tears cascading down my face.

You have no idea how much I love you and the amount of appreciation I have for you. I simply want to say thank you. Thank you for choosing to give me life. Thank you for birthing me. Thank you for being my Mother. Every struggle, every sacrifice you ever made to make sure that my siblings and I were taken care of, makes me value you all the more. I often look back in time and think about how much hard work and effort you put into taking care of your family. I know that it was no easy task, but ever since I was child, I have watched you take control and make things happen. As a child, I also watched you endure some of the most difficult times. I've seen your pain, your tears. I've witnessed you triumph through it all. You have shown me what it means to be a Mother who provides, a Mother who survives. You are a true example. You're a warrior. I can only hope to be half of the woman you are. There is no love like yours. You taught me that in this life, there will be ups and downs, but to remain steadfast. You told me to walk with my head held high so that God's love, power and strength can shine on me for when those tough times arise. Every time I think about it, my eyes fill with tears. I will never claim to be the most innocent child, but I truly hope that I've done something in this lifetime to make you proud. I cherish every encouraging word you've ever given me and every hug you've embraced me with. I'm so Blessed and fortunate to be able to have you here on this earth with me.

I love you so much.

My Prayer

Heavenly Father, I pray for the individual who has taken the time to read my words. I pray that my words captured their spirit and they were encouraged and enlightened. Father, please give them the tenacity to hold on to you and your words. We know that your word stands true and you reign forever. Even in the midst of darkness, Father, you are able to lift us up and sustain us. Please allow me to be a beacon of hope for the soul that reads the words I have written. Use me, Father. Write your word on my heart, so that I never forget it and help me to pour into a soul. This my prayer, that I ask in Your name. Amen. *"Therefore, shall ye lay up these words in your heart and in your soul, and bind them for a sign upon your hand, that they may be as frontlets between your eyes."* **Deuteronomy 11:18**

"But they that wait upon the Lord shall renew their strength; they shall mount up with wings as eagles; they shall run, and not be weary; and they shall walk, and not faint." **Isaiah 40:31**

You're Worth It

To the person who is reading this, **YOUR LIFE IS WORTH LIVING**. If you don't receive anything else from this, please know that you have value and you have worth. You have a reason to live. Anything or anyone who isn't adding value to your well-being, doesn't deserve occupancy. You are deserving of peace. Sometimes you have to walk alone. But with God by your side, you never have to worry about being alone. You have to do this for YOU, not your family or your friends. This is YOUR journey. Your life has purpose. Your life is valuable and it has meaning. Don't let anyone tell you different. There will be days of struggle. Keep in mind that, every day is a Blessing and another opportunity to win. The only way to see what is on the other side of the door, is to get up and walk towards it. You may experience setbacks. It will seem like you are failing and things aren't getting better. But stay rooted in Him and His Holy Word. GOD HAS NOT FORGOTTEN ABOUT YOU. He never will.

"They are like trees planted along a riverbank, with roots that reach deep into the water. Such trees are not bothered by the heat or worried by long months of drought. Their leaves stay green, and they never stop producing fruit." **Jeremiah 17:8 (NLT)**

"But those who trust in the Lord will find new strength. They will soar high on wings like eagles. They will run and not grow weary. They will walk and not faint." **Isaiah 40:31 (NLT)**

Dear Heavenly Father,

Thank You. Thank You for life---for it is such a precious gift. May I never take it for granted. Thank You for the Blessings You have graciously bestowed upon me. Thank You for the Blessings that are soon to come. This road can be rocky at times. I ask that You keep me near. My life has purpose. Because of your existence, Your sacrifice and Your love, I am here. I choose to live and to spend the rest of my days Glorifying Your name.

Amen.

Your Daughter, Lenisha

***I wanted to express my gratitude and say thank you to the following people:

White Boots 101 Writing Services LLC

(editing and publishing)

Mizrakli Photography

Emek Kiziltas (cover and illustration)

Niconna Johnson (The Dymond Beauty Brand

Ltd.) Makeup artist

CPSIA information can be obtained
at www.ICGtesting.com
Printed in the USA
BVHW050349110321
602124BV00017BB/1135